Advice for Young Musicians

Advice for Young Musicians

Ian Howell

Embodied Music Lab Press
Ann Arbor, Michigan

Copyright © 2023 by Ian Howell

All rights reserved. No part of this publication may be reproduced, distributed, or transmitted in any form or by any means, including photocopying, recording, or other electronic or mechanical methods, without the prior written permission of the publisher, except in the case of brief quotations embodied in critical reviews and certain other noncommercial uses permitted by copyright law.

ISBN: 979-8-9891865-0-1

Library of Congress Control Number: 2023919638

Published by Embodied Music Lab Press
Ann Arbor, Michigan, USA
www.embodiedmusiclab.com

For information about permission to reproduce selections from this book, write to: office@embodiedmusiclab.com

Back cover photograph credit: Andrew Hurlbut

First Edition: 2023

10 9 8 7 6 5 4 3 2 1

DEDICATION

To my teachers, and their teachers, and their teachers before them. And my students, and their students, and their students after them.

CONTENTS

	Foreword	i
	Introduction	iii
1	How Careers Unfold	1
2	How Music, Practice, and Performance Work	17
3	Business, Networking, and Relationships	40
4	Becoming Who You Are	65
5	Necessary Skills, Behaviors, and Outlooks	83
6	Academia and Education	97
7	Mentors and Teachers	110
	Appendix of Influences	126
	About the Author	127

FOREWORD

Sometimes in life, roles reverse in the most unexpected ways. In 2013, I had the privilege of mentoring Ian Howell, then a voice teacher in the NATS Intern program. Far from a conventional student, Ian brought with him experience as a former member of Chanticleer, not to mention his breathtaking countertenor voice. What struck me the most was the way Ian introduced us to the electronic visualization of the voice. There he was, analyzing singers in our intimate group with his tablet, delving into the intricacies of harmonics, formants, and sine waves, sharing his infectious curiosity with the rest of us. Through him, I witnessed the voice in a way I had never imagined.

When the world grappled with the challenges of the Covid-19 Pandemic, it was Ian's pioneering work in tackling latency and disseminating information that made high-quality virtual voice lessons possible. His adept integration of emerging technologies showcased not just technical prowess, but also an indomitable spirit of innovation. Further, his profound insights in psychoacoustics have sparked unprecedented discussions, questions, and explorations.

Ian's generosity knows no bounds. He constantly disseminates his knowledge, presenting at respected conferences and workshops like PAVA, NATS, the Voice Foundation, and the Acoustic Vocal Pedagogy Workshop. Many admire him for his ability to provoke thoughtful discourse.

In *Advice for Young Musicians*, Ian is not merely providing tips. He is challenging young musicians and their mentors to think deeply about their craft, the realities of their profession, self-discovery, and the very ethos of music-making. Phrases like "amazing average," "almost all work comes from work," and "breathe and smile for three seconds" ask readers to explore layers of meaning and purpose.

This is more than a book. It's an invitation to journey into the heart of what it truly means to grow in a life in music.

Karen Brunssen
Professor of Voice
Co-Chair of Music Performance
Bienen School of Music, Northwestern University
14 October 2023
Evanston, Illinois

INTRODUCTION

At different times in my career as an instrumentalist, singer, and educator, I have wanted very different things for myself. As a result, I have had the chance to thoroughly live several different musical identities. Some of these identities facilitated true peak career experiences — recording for major labels and traveling the world, working as a soloist in spaces like Carnegie Hall, and designing and teaching a bespoke graduate voice pedagogy degree program at the New England Conservatory. Other identities have humbled and challenged me and caused me to doubt what might come next. Through all these experiences, the words of my own mentors continue to ring in my mind, as is popular to say now, *rent free*. These voices encourage, challenge, chide, and console in equal measure.

This book offers ideas for navigating the world as a musician. Some are paraphrases of advice given to me by a specific person, and the appendix offers credit where it is due. Much of this book is a simple distillation of patterns that I was fortunate enough to remain in the music industry long enough to see. Read it front to back, dip in and out, dog-ear pages that speak to you, or argue with what I share here. As you grow as a person and as a musician, the advice on these pages will take on different meanings at different times. I hope these thoughts spark your imagination and save you time and heartache as you make your own way. At minimum, I hope you will see that you are alone in neither your successes nor your struggles.

Ian Howell
17 September 2023
Ann Arbor, Michigan

1

HOW CAREERS UNFOLD

We cannot expect that the arts institutions we grew up aware of will provide employment when our turn comes. Build a network, make opportunities for yourself and others, and market yourself. Sell yourself to different people in different ways.

Use whatever technology you can to create communities around your projects. Whatever technologies your teachers suggest are likely already out of date.

Ian Howell

It is unlikely that you are a revolutionary, paradigm-shifting artist, that you will get your big break doing only what you love, or that the industry will reward you financially for making new music. So, learn how to play music that people older than you already like to listen to, even if you would rather not. Performing older music for people older than you is far more likely to give you the economic freedom to do what you *actually* want to do. You can make more money playing well-known songs as background music in a restaurant for a few hours over the weekend than you can working at a service job or in retail.

It is one thing to be told that paths to success are non-linear. It is another thing to live it. Even a circuitous path looks like a path in retrospect. Prospectively, it always looks like a cliff in the near distance.

Ian Howell

Always have a project in the planning stages, another you are almost ready for, a third you are actively producing, and a fourth in the rear-view mirror. If other people are not providing you with these opportunities, create them yourself.

Few people have career-catalyzing events like a big competition win, a prestigious training program, or a high-profile award. Most who do, do not capitalize on these experiences. Waiting for a career windfall is a bad Plan A, and most working musicians get work by working. So, if that sort of thing does not work out for you, it probably will not impact your long-term viability.

Ian Howell

Any portion of the music industry that made space for you as a young musician will continue to make space for other young musicians as you age. Figure out how to remain in those circles if you can, but do not come to resent the process that gave you a chance.

No one wants to hear it, but the ultimate power you have over an unworkable situation is to leave. You will not solve every conflict. You will not right every wrong.

Ian Howell

Success rarely feels like success when it happens to you. Every one of your idols is currently anxious about whether their next season is fully booked.

Being a featured soloist pays more than being an ensemble member, but it is lonely. Being an ensemble member pays less, but the work is steady.

Everything great in this world exists because someone decided to make it happen. That person is most likely not smarter, more talented, or more innovative than you. Let that empower you. You get to do it too.

There is nothing like having a prominent conductor, producer, intendant, or band leader love your singing or playing. If you are not performing for them, they cannot hear you. If you do not move in their circles, and they will not take your audition, offer to pay them to coach you.

Musicians are far more dependent on the disposable income of others than other tradespeople or craftspeople. Unless the arts funding climate in your country is robust, there will be mass extinction events in your industry in your lifetime. Be prepared to recognize the signs of this sort of industry-wide reshuffling — for example, if musicians more famous and successful than you become affordable to the groups you usually work with. You cannot fight this. It is bigger than you. Do your best to weather these times with humility.

Very few people owe you an explanation. Unless you are paying someone else for their time, you will most likely have to figure out what they think of you based on their actions.

If there is a city you want to work in regularly, seriously consider moving there. If you imagine you can just fly in for auditions, you will miss all the local auditions and the word-of-mouth connections that *actually* allow you to network and work in that scene.

2

HOW MUSIC, PRACTICE, AND PERFORMANCE WORK

Ian Howell

There is no such thing as technical work separate from expressive performance. You have no idea what your technical needs are until you know what you want to say when you perform.

The technical competencies your teachers keep mentioning — how to blend with others, what clear diction or articulation feels like, how loud or quiet you must be, that small notes are agents of larger shapes, etc. — are the things that professionals remember to do all the time. Some of your practical work is about gaining a new coordination, learning important ideas, or repeatedly trying until something awkward is comfortable. However, the bulk of your work is remembering to remember.

World-class performers are not perfect. They make mistakes. What separates them from the rest of the pack is the quality and consistency of their average performance. They have a strong B Game. Remember that as you practice; your goal is an amazing average (rather than a continuous peak) performance.

No matter what you do, no matter what feedback a teacher gives you, the most likely result every time you try to make music is your average performance. This means that negative reinforcement will appear to help when you make a mistake, because your next attempt will likely rise to your average performance, and your average is better than the mistake. Positive reinforcement will appear to hinder when you do exceptionally well, because you will likely regress from that peak back to your average performance. This is especially true when a task is new, and your execution is inconsistent. The sooner your approach to practice relieves you of the need to receive what is frequently irrelevant feedback, the sooner you will improve the quality and consistency of your average performance.

Ian Howell

In your practice and performance, let the two possible outcomes be either radical success or catastrophic failure. No one ever moved people by first protecting themselves from the mistakes they are afraid they will make.

If you are a singer or a melodic instrumentalist, learn a chordal instrument and vice versa. Music is almost always horizontal and vertical at the same time.

Ian Howell

Musical expression is rarely captured more efficiently with words than it is with music. In a rehearsal, never explain how you would like a colleague to phrase something. Always show them with your voice or with your instrument.

"Healthy technique" does not have an aesthetic. Healthy means dependable, sustainable, and repeatable. It is common to find teachers unable to teach or perform certain techniques in a healthy manner. That is generally a story about the teacher, not necessarily a story about whether the technique promotes health.

It is common to find musicians wary of imitating others, but those who can imitate well have learned to listen.

Historically, most music performance settings outside the Church have involved alcohol and socializing. If you want to meet people where they are, they are at a bar. Most truly imaginative, delightful, and surprising music makes more sense if you imagine the audience is at least a little tipsy.

In tonal music, some vertical sonorities feel content and self-complete while others seem to long for a resolution to other sounds. The fewer extensions (7ths, 9ths, etc.) and the closer the bass note is to the root of the chord, the more stable the sonority. Play the harmony in this way, and your individual role in the corporate expression will be clear.

Every notated music tradition uses its own shorthand and leverages a set of assumptions regarding what the performer will bring to the page. This means it is supposed to feel spontaneous, even when it is written down.

Sound and life comes in waves. Play music like that and people will understand even if they do not understand.

It is only oppositions that move the human soul. Play the contrasts.

Practice slow crescendos and decrescendos on sustained tones. You will rarely do it in performance, but this skill means that you can do it across an extended series of pitches in a melody. This is the core technical competency that allows you to phrase with style.

Linear analysis (typically associated with Schenker's work) is either taught as a reductive analytical approach, completely disconnected from expression and performance rhetoric, or it is taught as an incredibly elegant way to understand how to perform tonal music. Prejudge it at your own peril. A good linear analysis teacher will be able to play or sing examples to demonstrate how the rhetorical shapes of the simpler harmonic and melodic reductions generate the musical expression of the surface melody.

It must be important that the bass figures in Baroque and Classical music performance scores never include Roman numerals. If the composers and performers did not use that notation, why do we analyze their music in this way?

Approach the analysis of structural design in music as if you are a listener with pain in their life, not a spectator with a calculator. The ii$^6_5$ does not voice lead mathematically to the V$_7$ and then to the I. Tension in a musical sound progresses to a resolution that reflects actual tension and release that we feel in our physical bodies. These sounds glue to one another to create a larger sense of being drawn to an arrival point. Figure out that path so that you can perform it as though you are creating the music spontaneously.

Virtuosity and expressivity are not bound to a single place, time, tradition, or culture.

Music is inextricably tied to culture, but only because cultures read that music into the present through their own lens. This means the same music can mean different things at different times. Or it can mean different things to different cultures at the same time. Almost all music has a long and complicated history. This tells a story about the eras it has moved through as much as the specific culture it emerged from. Do not pretend that there is only the present, and only your culture.

Unlike a marble sculpture or an oil painting, one must choose to remake a work of music for it to continue to exist. Remaking music in the present moment can be audacious, offensive, profound, or redemptive in a way that looking at a statue is not.

There is a robust and expanding field of study that addresses how to practice efficiently and how we master complex motor tasks. Your applied teacher will most likely not be aware of this research.

3

BUSINESS, NETWORKING, AND RELATIONSHIPS

Prioritize understanding contracts. Always ask whether it is a *favored nations* fee structure. This means all the soloists or ensemble members are paid the same amount. If not, always ask if your fee can be improved. If you are contracting the gig, tell your musicians upfront when everyone is making the same amount. Transparency breeds buy-in.

If you must turn down a gig because you have another one on the books, keep in mind that this transmits your desirability to the declined party. Graciously ask them to keep you in mind for future opportunities.

It is almost always better to follow through with the gig you currently have booked rather than to cancel for a seemingly better one. The only exception that does not burn bridges in this dynamic is when the better opportunity makes the group you back out on appear important by association.

Ian Howell

Sometimes you burn bridges. There are always more bridges out there, but do not make it a habit.

A music training tradition that has formally located itself within academia will tend to generate a pipeline of post-graduate training programs, workshops, and competitions. These run the gamut from paid to free to tuition-based. Anyone within that academia-to-training-program pipeline (and often back to academia) will be inundated by advertising for these programs, which creates the impression that they are the path to a professional career. To be sure, these training programs may teach important skills and help one build a network of peers. However, every industry has a far less visible group of professionals that *actually* hire musicians. Band leaders, artistic administrators, intendants, conductors, and the like make careers. They do not need to advertise. Do not confuse the training industry for the actual industry.

Outside of church choirs and academic programs, I can count on one hand the number of auditions I sang that led directly to a gig. Almost all work comes from work.

Respond first to the e-mails that will generate the most future income.

Aim for the middle of your industry. That is where the steady money is.

If you can, make a list of five mid-industry performers ten years ahead of you in the business. Use them as case studies. Figure out when they worked with what groups and reason through how they navigated their career. Then, map out how to slowly take their gigs. Not out of malice. Wish them better gigs.

If you have a hard time finding examples of mid-level artists ten years older than you, ask whether there was some sort of economic cataclysm. If you have problems finding examples of mid-level artists twenty years older than you, consider whether your industry has a future.

If you can, get two colleagues to casually mention you to someone you would like to work for within the span of a few weeks. This triangulation works better than repeatedly cold calling or emailing. If you do not have two colleagues who have worked with that target person, make it your goal to triangulate on the gigs that will make those connections. This part of your career may last years. It may always be like this.

It is incredibly unlikely that you are an example of the type of student you will attract. This does not mean you have failed. It means they need something different than you did. Set your fee based on the value you provide your students, not as a percentage of what you pay your own teacher. This means it is ok to charge more than your teacher charges you.

Advancing in the industry often means saying no to offers you would have previously accepted. Say no to these colleagues with compassion. Even if you do not want to work with that group anymore, you want them to seek out your students in the future.

Celebrate the success of your colleagues even if (especially if) you want what they have.

Your first goal on a gig should be to get rehired. You do this by solving problems and being easy to work with. Your second goal should be to network with colleagues on that gig so that someone mentions you as an option for another gig. It can take years for those contacts to convert to a contract, so make a lot of them.

Ian Howell

Be the person who makes rehearsals run smoothly. Of course, be prepared. But, also be present, supportive, and ready to change the plan you brought into the space. Make something new and wonderful.

The most visible performers are the ones who pay public relations teams to talk about them. This is expensive. Most working musicians do their own marketing. Someone viewing the business from the outside may point to these high visibility musicians as examples of success and suggest that anything short of this kind of visibility is a failure.

People will tell you that you must do x, y, or z to market yourself. Play to your strengths. If you are good at being quirky on social media, do that. If you are not yet a skilled writer, do not start a blog. If you cannot create good performance videos, do not publish bad ones. Self-marketing must reflect who you actually are, even if that image is curated.

Almost no one in a position of power thinks they have power. Be kind to others if there is money involved.

Ian Howell

Almost no one in a position to hire trusts their own opinion. Make it easy for other people to talk about how great you are and how easy you are to work with.

Some people are not great at dealing with conflict in a professional setting. If this is you, let your first reaction to a tense situation be to breathe and smile for three seconds.

Ian Howell

The music industry is made up of gently connected networks. You are unlikely to jump to a better paying, more prestigious, more rewarding network until it is obvious that you are better than everyone around you. This means the central goal of your daily practice must be to move toward personal excellence. Every day will present hundreds of chances to be pulled away from that, but it is the core of your business.

If you resent your professional network and cannot access better opportunities, pay someone you trust for an honest evaluation of how you are performing. It is important that you pay them.

Be on the lookout for survivorship bias. If someone tells you that you must accomplish x before you can accomplish y, it is likely they are sharing their biography rather than a universal truth.

4

BECOMING WHO YOU ARE

Ian Howell

Do not try to be the second anyone. It is enough to be the first you.

Read Coleman Barks' translations of Rumi's poetry about music and longing.

If you know that you want your life to be different ten years from now, take concrete steps starting today.

Set goals and work toward them. Let some of those goals be the lofty answers to the question: "How do I want the world to be different for my having lived in it?" No one ever unintentionally changed the world. Let some of those goals be the practical answers to the question: "What can I get done tomorrow?" Every massive project began with the first actionable task.

Ian Howell

Recordings are not performances. Go wild.

It is ok to change your mind about what you want to do with your life. Just because you are good at something does not mean you have to do it for money. Just because someone else was better than you when you were young does not mean you will not exceed them in time. Just because you did something well when you were young does not mean you cannot set it aside as you age. Just because you had a good reason to do something when you were younger does not make it right for you now. Just because you did something for the wrong reason before does not mean you cannot do it for a better reason now.

If you are good at more than one thing, keep doing them all until the world tells you what to put down and what to prioritize. You will know what to choose based on where your money comes from.

There is a difference between what you can execute as a performer and what you can hear. The best performers — even world-class musicians — are typically able to hear their own imperfections even when others cannot. In practical terms, this means that no matter your success, you will always be aware of what could be better. This is normal.

Ian Howell

There is nothing to talk about until there is something to talk about. Try to write your ideas down and you will learn whether you understand them.

The only thorough critique of a flawed analysis is a better analysis. Engaging in this process will help you understand how hard it is to put your work out into the world.

Ian Howell

You need more sleep.

You do not need to be the same person on stage as you are in real life. You do not even need to use the same name. You do not need to reconcile these two aspects of yourself.

Ultimately, you will come to your daily practice routine for your own reasons. It is normal to do it for another person's reasons when you are younger, but those people will retire and die. Continuing for their memory alone gives the dead a veto over the decisions of the living. The process of discovering why you want to keep going takes time, but the sooner you begin that process, the better.

There is no such thing as a single truth about you as a performing artist. You will not be universally validated. Someone will always refuse to hire you. It is not personal.

It is ok to love the music that you sing or play and not want to sing or play (or even enjoy) other styles. This is not disrespectful. It is ok to want to be a specialist. It is also ok to be a generalist.

Everyone ultimately plateaus. If you are unhappy with where you end up, it is ok to do something else with your life.

There is nothing about insight gained at a young age that is intrinsically superior to insight gained at an older age. Most people who achieve their goals early in life get bored and quit anyway.

5

NECESSARY SKILLS, BEHAVIORS, AND OUTLOOKS

If you cannot find new music, rehearse effectively with a collaborator, and mount a performance in thirty days without a coach or teacher, you have un-remediated deficiencies. If you cannot get people to show up to a performance on thirty days' notice, you need to expand your network. Start going to other peoples' shows and say hello after.

Holding on to anger is like holding onto a hot coal while planning on throwing it at someone else. You are the one getting burned.

Unless you are in danger, when you say the Big Yes to a project, you give up the right to say the little no a thousand times along the way. Instead say the Big No the next time you are offered that kind of project.

If you die on every hill, you are the one dying.

Make a lot of friends with people who work on the same kinds of gigs as you do, but in a different capacity. If you are a sax player and you must back out on a commitment, the leader is going to ask for recommendations to replace you from all the non-sax players left on the gig.

No music or musical role is beneath you, especially if it pays and you need the money.

Do not try to teach until you decide to try to be good at teaching.

You cannot teach somebody who does not want to learn.

Never give unsolicited advice to a colleague on a gig. Your job is to make them feel like they can shine around you. Your job is to make their job easier.

You either have more time or more money. This will change as you get older. Spend what you have more of.

Technologies that your mentors never used will come to dominate the day-to-day management of your career. This includes obvious tools like website builders, social media, email lists, and online commerce. Less obvious are the low latency, high-quality online music collaboration tools, audio interfaces, and microphones that will allow you to reorganize the way you rehearse, study, and teach. Even if you only want to make acoustic music, take the time to learn how to use these professional tools. This will save you thousands of dollars in travel and lodging expenses and enable collaborations that would have otherwise been cost-prohibitive.

There is nothing intrinsically better about musicians who can read music, but it makes them more employable.

It takes courage to start improvising, but nothing is more important for your musicianship.

6

ACADEMIA AND EDUCATION

The point of getting an education is to change; be brave enough to welcome that.

The term "gap year" assumes that formal schooling is our natural state. It is not. Only start a degree if you understand why you need to be changed in the way that the degree will change you. A university is an expensive place to figure out what you want from an education. If you want to be a musician, go out into your community and make music. Do not worry, you will learn whether you need more education.

Academic institutions will center a set of values that reflect their investments. A school with an expensive building will expect you to value the resources in that expensive building. A school with a dormitory will prioritize the power of a residential education. A school with a faculty disconnected from the current music industry will value the memory of the past. You will never own those buildings; you will never have a time machine. Take what you can, but make sure your personal values are not limited by the priorities of large institutions.

Music schools are frequently organized to appeal to what underinformed, prospective students imagine the music industry is. This can influence curriculum, faculty composition, and strategic initiatives. Often, this means pushing a narrative that (1) high-visibility, high-profile performance careers are widely attainable and (2) that anything falling short of these outcomes is a failure. If a school offers you many ways to learn who you are and what you might want to explore as a professional musician, matriculate. If a school prioritizes fantasy over gaining the skills needed to enter the actual music industry, run. You can simultaneously aim for artistry and employability.

If you are in a degree program, stay laser-focused on what you will do the day after graduation. On that day, very little of what held your passionate attention will still be relevant. Very few of the perceived slights you endured will still matter.

Music schools must do more than *conserve* culture. They must also reflect and comment upon contemporary culture. Beware of a curriculum with requirements solely based on keeping traditions alive for their own sake.

Music education may touch on many aspects of culture, but it must ultimately teach you how music works. If you have only been trained to perform a very narrow slice of repertory in specific performance contexts — how to be a cog in a very specific kind of machine — it is possible that you did not receive a complete music education. If your education did not teach you to spontaneously compose music that sounds idiomatic in your performance genres, it is unlikely that you will perform the works of others with spontaneity.

Beware of the training program that only leads to more training programs.

Ian Howell

In academic power structures, the person able to make others wait is the person in charge.

Anyone who tears down Genre A to build up Genre B likely does not understand Genre A, even if they say they do.

Academia is wonderful, but it is not representative of the real performance industry. The real performing world is wonderful, but encountering curious people interested in your growth is rare.

It is only in academia that portions of the music industry are pitted against each other (for example, classical versus contemporary, opera versus musical theater, orchestras versus chamber music). It is primarily because your physical footprint on campus is a 1:1 sign of your value to the institution. Only in that sort of environment does prioritizing one kind of music mean diminishing the resources allocated to another.

7

MENTORS AND TEACHERS

In the best-case scenario, people give advice based on their lived experience. Often, they give advice to justify their choices, personal outcomes, or resentments. Make sure that you listen to the advice of those who had positive, neutral, and negative experiences in school, in the business, and in life. While it is easier to find negative voices in public spaces, know that they are typically overrepresented.

Ian Howell

In a lesson, the person doing the most talking is often the person doing the most learning. The person making the most music is the person getting better at making music.

The best teachers ultimately want to mentor you to the point that you are their professional colleague. The further you progress in your education, the more likely this transition becomes. Eventually, it may appear as though you hit a point where your teacher stops pushing you and instead treats you like a colleague with something to say. They have not given up on you. They recognize that their work is done, and that they get to enjoy collaborating with you as a professional. This is not inevitable but enjoy it when it happens.

Parents and teachers will let you down once you see them as real people. Remember: that is a story about you, not them.

Mentors, like anyone else, have their own skill sets. If they work within academia, it is likely that they will prioritize the value of that skill set (and devalue other skills) as an act of self-preservation. No one survives in academia by suggesting that students need something they are unable to provide. This means that it is common for mentors to push *you* to stay within *their* comfort zone. The mentor interested in your growth is the mentor willing to grow.

You likely need three different teachers over your career: one to give you love, love for the music, and encouragement; one to give you the technique you need to survive; and one to transmit the performance tradition. Sometimes this is the same person. Most of the time it is not. None of these teachers have failed you just because they only offered what they could.

Singers and instrumentalists will experience performance-related injuries and impairments, most often through no fault of their own. If a teacher creates a culture that stigmatizes these performance injuries, their students will delay seeking the treatment and therapy they need.

Many older teachers were raised in a culture that presumed that students want whatever their teachers want for them. If your teacher has not asked you what your goals are, tell them what you want as a person, as a musician, and as a member of your various communities. If you have students, prompt this conversation before working on anything else. There is no use in wasting time working with someone who cannot buy into your goals.

It is ok to not want the career that your teacher thinks is *the best*. They are likely older than you and do not understand what entry-level work is in the current music industry. Try to be as successful as they were, but it will almost certainly be by doing different things.

Most of what passes for applied pedagogy today is storytelling. Your teacher will tell you how to breathe, for example, by sharing a story about how their teacher told them to breathe. Surprisingly, most performers are not actually doing what they think they are with their body, and it is difficult to verify compliance with these stories beyond satisfaction with the result. Always ask yourself: *Is thinking in this way helping me*, not *is what they are saying true?*

Barring an impairment, we demonstrate that we understand a musical or technical concept by executing it, not by explaining it with words. If your teacher does not bring you to the experience of *doing the thing yourself*, you have not learned it.

There is no meaningful litmus test for a prospective teacher beyond whether they can teach you. Do not rent time with a famous person who will make you feel temporarily important, but who can neither help you nor give you relevant career connections.

If a teacher or coach's intake process requires that you share an enemy before you make music, they are trying to manipulate you emotionally for their financial gain.

Ian Howell

Sometimes a teacher and student are a bad match. This does not mean the teacher cannot teach others or that the student cannot learn. While it is difficult to change studios in some academic settings, the self-awareness that a change is needed is a necessary professional skill. If you cannot tell whether someone you are paying to help you improve is helping you improve, imagine how hard it will be to advocate for your needs in the professional world.

Almost everyone you encounter has something to offer. If you can, do not let the ways in which they fall short of what you think you need stop you from learning what they can give you.

APPENDIX OF INFLUENCES

22	My late voice teacher, Lynne Vardaman
24	This is a trait I observed in highly effective conductors like Jeffrey Thomas, John Scott, Simon Carrington, and Kent Tritle.
28	This is a reflection on the way that Dr. Joan Panetti, Emerita Professor of Music at Yale University, described how composers use harmonic "glue" to structure musical sounds.
30	Based on the analytical philosophy of Robert Cogan, late Emeritus Professor of Composition and Theoretical Analysis at New England Conservatory
31	Paraphrase from the introduction to Claudio Monteverdi's *Book Eight of Madrigals*
52	One of many important ideas related to pricing I learned in music business consulting with Michelle Markwart Deveaux
55	Paraphrase of colleague and baritone Jesse Blumberg
61	I first observed this behavior from Matthew Oltman when we sang together in Chanticleer
66	My late mother, Susan Howell
70	My late father, John Howell
72	Paraphrase of Ronald Cook, former director of the Early Interval
74	Paraphrase of comments made by Dr. Helen Greenwald, Professor of Music History and Musicology at New England Conservatory
75	Paraphrase of comments made by Robert Cogan, late Emeritus Professor of Composition and Theoretical Analysis at New England Conservatory
82	Paraphrase of advice shared by Stan Smith, Professor of Jazz Guitar at Capital University
84	Inspired by David Taylor's Handbook for the Professional Singer
85	Attributed to the Buddha

ABOUT THE AUTHOR

Dr. Ian Howell is the founder of and chief educator at the Embodied Music Lab. He has held classroom and studio teaching appointments at the New England Conservatory of Music, the Cleveland Institute of Music, Yale College, Swarthmore, and Rutgers. He has sung in most major concert halls across America, Europe, Canada, and Japan as a soloist and with numerous professional ensembles. He has presented original research on performing arts biodynamics at the National Association of Teachers of Singing (NATS), the Pan American Vocology Association (PAVA), the Voice Foundation, the Audio Engineering Society, and the Society for Music Perception and Cognition, and has peer reviewed for Oxford University Press, the International Physiology & Acoustics of Singing Conference (PAS7+), Musicae Scientiae, and PAVA. Ian has been an invited guest speaker and clinician for the NATS Chat series, the New York Singing Teacher's Association, Opera Programs Berlin, Peabody Lunch and Learn, Mannes, CU Boulder, New York University, Boston Conservatory, and the San Francisco Conservatory. He is published in the Journal of Voice, the Journal of Singing, Classical Singer, and VOICEPrints. He has won professional recognitions ranging from a Grammy Award and a Grammy Award Nomination for his recordings with Chanticleer to a special commendation by the American Academy of Teachers of Singing for his "work with low-latency platforms and associated technology, and broad dissemination of instruction in its use" during the Covid 19 pandemic. Ian won the Van L. Lawrence Fellowship in 2022 for work investigating cis male bias in a common voice science model, and he was elected to the American Academy of Teachers of Singing in 2023. His research interests include the intersection of human perception and the singing voice with a special focus on the role of auditory transduction. He now reaches a worldwide audience of clients and students via high-quality, low-latency online collaboration tools. He holds degrees in music from Capital University, Yale University, and the New England Conservatory of Music.

Ian Howell lives in Ann Arbor, Michigan with his wife and their two children. There is talk of getting a cat.